# Helping Your
## Transgender Teen

# Helping Your
# Transgender Teen

## A Guide for Parents

# Irwin Krieger

GENDERWISE
PRESS

NEW HAVEN

The information and suggestions contained in this book are not intended as a substitute for consulting directly with a mental health clinician. All matters regarding your child's physical and mental health require professional supervision. The author and publisher shall not be liable or responsible for any loss or damage caused or allegedly caused by any information or suggestion in this book.

Author photo by Thomas Hurlbut
www.thomashurlbutphotography.com

Published by Genderwise Press, New Haven.

ISBN: 069201229X
EAN-13: 9780692012291
LCCN: 2010941315

*For my parents,*
*Nava and Elbie,*
*in appreciation of your love and tenacity*
*during my own youthful push for authenticity*

# Acknowledgements

Thanks to the teens and parents who put their trust in me and taught me so much; to my partner, John Mayer, for your patience, support and encouragement, and for your astute advice through multiple drafts of this book; to Alan Krieger, Sena Messer, Lisa Taylor and Sharon Laura for your helpful suggestions and revisions; and to Lois Spivack, for your help and guidance in my work with transgender clients.

Thanks, also, to Kate Bornstein, Syracuse Cultural Workers, Matt Kailey, Ellen Wittlinger, Janis Astor del Valle, the loving parents of one very confident transgender teen, and the estates of James Baldwin and Eleanor Roosevelt for generously giving me permission to borrow your words.

# Contents

CHAPTER ONE

# INTRODUCTION

*In times of difficulty take refuge in compassion and truth.*
— Buddhist teaching

Today's teens have access to a wealth of information on the internet. Teenagers who are wondering about gender identity soon find out what it means to be transgender or transsexual. They watch video accounts of young people progressing through physical changes from hormones. They converse with other teens who share similar feelings about their identity. Parents, on the other hand, know little about this topic. Most have never considered that their child may be transgender. They are not prepared when their child begins to talk with them about it.

**How this book will help you**

If you are the parent of a transgender teen, this book will help you understand what your child is feeling and experiencing. It will explain what may be in store for you if your child fully embraces what it means to be transgender. Most parents do not know anyone who is transgender. They initially approach the subject with tremendous discomfort. It is extremely important as the parent of a transgender child to educate yourself about the variety of gender identities that exist. Be prepared to let go of some of your ideas about what it means to be male or female.

These ideas may have been shaped by your childhood. When you were growing up you learned what it meant to be a boy or a girl. Perhaps what you learned felt right to you and you never gave it much thought. Or perhaps there were times when you felt fenced in by what others expected of you because you were a girl, or because you were a boy. You may have been kept from certain activities or discouraged from pursuing certain interests because of your gender. Most likely by adulthood you figured out how to make your way in the world without questioning whether you are a woman or a man. If you are reading this book, however, someone you care about is struggling with questions about gender.

When a teenager declares he or she is transgender, parents fear that their child is confused and is choosing a life fraught with danger. As the parent of this teen, you will find it is best to be thoughtful, inquisitive and compassionate as you come to understand more about your child's gender identity.

**Why I wrote this book**

I am a clinical social worker who has been providing psychotherapy for lesbian, gay, bisexual and transgender (LGBT) individuals and their families for the past 25 years. In the past 7 years, my work has included more and more transgender teens and their parents. I want to share with you what I have learned from my years of working with these caring and courageous families.

Right now, you may be feeling confused, angry, highly skeptical or completely disbelieving that your child could be transgender. If so, this book is for you. In the next chapter I'll help you understand the words and ideas we use when we talk about gender identity. The following three chapters will highlight gender nonconforming children, the differences between gender and sexuality, and the challenges of adolescence for transgender kids. The remaining chapters will help you address your fears, concerns and uncertainties about your child, so you can be as supportive as possible while your child continues to explore questions about gender identity.

# CHAPTER TWO

# THE LANGUAGE OF GENDER IDENTITY

*There's a simple way to look at gender. Once upon a time, someone drew a line in the sands of culture and proclaimed with great self-importance, "On this side you are a man; on the other side you are a woman." It's time for the winds of change to blow that line away.*

— Kate Bornstein, *Gender Outlaw*

Let's begin by taking a close look at some of the words we use to describe our transgender teens. By understanding various components of personal identity, we can open a window on the inner lives of teens who question whether they are the boy or girl that others take them to be.

*Sex*, female or male, is assigned at birth based on the appearance of the baby's genitals. That seems pretty straightforward, and it is for the most part. But approximately one percent of babies are *intersex*; their genitals are not clearly male or female. For our discussion of transgender teens, we will begin with the idea that a person's sex is either male or female, based on body structure. But knowing about intersex people reminds us that categories such as male/female, gay/straight, or short/tall generally have an in-between.

*Gender identity* is a person's inner sense of being female, male, neither or both. Most people have a clear sense of being either male or female -- their gender identity conforms to their biological sex. Rules about how girls and boys should behave are taught to us by our families, peers, schools, books, movies, and other representations in the popular culture. These rules establish certain expectations for each gender.

*Gender expression* is a person's presentation of self to others as masculine, feminine, neither or both. The various attributes and behaviors that signal male or female vary somewhat from one national culture or ethnic group to another. Aspects of gender expression include one's manner of movement and speech, ways of dressing and grooming, and certain behaviors and interests that are considered to be acceptable only for girls (such as playing with dolls) or only for boys (such as playing football). Children whose gender presentation does not meet society's (and the family's) expectations for their biological sex generally are treated with disapproval. They learn quickly to try to change themselves to fit in. *Gender nonconforming* children are those who persist in their preferred behaviors and interests, even when those run counter to what is expected of them as a boy or a girl.

*Transgender* is a word that describes a wide variety of individuals. Most people are *conventionally gendered*: I use this term to mean that their sex, gender identity and gender expression are all male or all female. But transgender people have a gender identity and/or gender expression that does *not* conform to the sex of their body.

- *Transsexuals* (see below) are included under the transgender umbrella.

- Some transgender people have a gender identity that is neither male nor female, or is a blend of female and male. People with an in-between gender identity sometimes consider themselves to be *genderfluid* or *genderqueer*.

- Another group included under the transgender umbrella is people who cross dress. *Crossdressers* wish to adopt the clothing and styles of grooming typical, in their culture, of the other sex. They may or may not question their gender identity. They may or may not feel it is important to appear convincingly as the other sex when they are cross dressed.

*Transsexuals* are people whose gender identity is in sharp contrast to their biological sex. This may be expressed as being, for example, "a man in a woman's body." Another way to express this is to say that a teenager is a *transboy*, or an *affirmed male* whose biological sex is female. Most transgender teens who speak up about being transgender are transsexual. (Those who are genderfluid or crossdressers are more likely to handle this in secret or be seen as rebelling, unconventional or "just going through a phase.") While this book will focus primarily on the experiences of transsexual teens, most of the information also applies to transgender teens who are genderfluid, genderqueer or crossdressers but not transsexual.

Transsexuals are unhappy with the aspects of their bodies that do not conform to the gender they feel they are inside. You may have heard the term *gender dysphoria*. This term is used to describe the unhappiness caused by the conflict between gender identity and biological sex or societal expectations for that sex.

- a *male-to-female* (MTF) transsexual has a male body, is considered by others to be male, but feels she is female. She wants to have a female body and to be viewed by others as female. (Using female pronouns, in this instance, is consistent with how this person feels about herself, despite starting out in life with a male body and appearance.)

- A *female-to-male* (FTM) transsexual has a female body but feels he is male. He wants to have a male body and to be viewed by others as male. (Using the pronouns that correspond to a person's gender identity is a sign of respect. I will discuss this further in Chapters 8 and 9 when I discuss the social transition.)

Is this getting confusing? Imagine, then, what it is like growing up without any words or role models to explain feeling female but having a male body. Or being told you are a girl when you know inside you are a boy. Most transsexuals grow up feeling different from other kids. They don't fit in. Let's take a look at these gender nonconforming children in the next chapter.

## CHAPTER THREE

# GENDER NONCONFORMING KIDS

*For every girl who throws out her E-Z Bake Oven,*
*There is a boy who wishes to find one.*
— From "Every Girl Every Boy" by J.T. Bunnell and Irit Reinheim,
Adapted from "For Every Woman" by Nancy R. Smith.

Gender nonconforming (GNC) kids don't have it easy. They are the boys who want to play with dolls and don't like rough and tumble activities. Or the girls who won't wear a dress and want to play with the boys. GNC kids like to dress as the opposite sex and take on opposite sex roles in fantasy play. GNC boys may be teased for effeminate mannerisms or high-pitched voices. GNC girls are not interested in jewelry, make-up and frills. They are interested in cars, trucks and team sports. Girls are less likely to be teased, because they fit in the socially accepted "tomboy" role.

Most parents are at ease with a girl who is a tomboy, as long as she conforms to gender expectations at times and grows out of being a tomboy by the time she is a young woman. But the feminine boy is a difficult challenge for his parents. They worry that others will ridicule him, and perhaps think less of them as well. They fear that he is a "sissy" or a "momma's boy." It's hard for some parents to be proud of their feminine son, because of strong cultural taboos against effeminacy. Parents usually encourage these boys to tone down the feminine aspects of their interests and behaviors. To some extent, they also encourage their tomboys to pursue more feminine interests.

### GNC kids don't fit in easily

GNC kids have a strong sense of not fitting in. At ages when girls play mostly with girls and boys with boys, the GNC child is more comfortable with opposite sex playmates. The boy who plays with girls may be looked down on by his peers and by some adults. The girl who wants to play with the boys may be told "No girls allowed!" GNC kids are more likely than gender conforming children to be teased, insulted and rejected by peers and adults. They may sense that they are a disappointment to the adults who matter the most to them, including parents and teachers. They find few if any role models in the popular culture, and often struggle with low self-esteem. GNC kids who lack social and family support may feel a tremendous sense of shame. They are at great risk of depression, social isolation, self-harm or suicide

### Which GNC kids grow up to be transsexual?

Most GNC children grow up to be gay, lesbian or bisexual. Some will be gender nonconforming heterosexual adults (but other people may wonder if they are gay or lesbian because of their manner and interests.) And some will be transgender teens and adults. The more strongly gender nonconforming children are the most likely to be transsexual in adulthood. A strongly GNC boy is one who says out loud that he really is a girl, that he was given the wrong body. He may express dislike for his penis and sit down when urinating. A strongly GNC girl may believe she will grow up to be a man. She may want to wear boys' underwear and keep her hair short. She may express a wish for a penis and dislike developing breasts. She will not celebrate getting her period and becoming a woman. Strongly GNC boys may feel they should keep their chest covered, always wearing a shirt at the pool or the beach. The girls may want to run around without a shirt on long past the age when parents think it's okay. Children whose strong gender nonconformance persists from year to year are most likely to grow up to be transsexual.

## Was your teen GNC in childhood?

Think back to when your son or daughter was a young child. Do you recall whether he or she exhibited many of these gender nonconforming behaviors and desires? Take a look at family photos and videos to see whether your child's public presentation reflected this difference. Do you remember any time your son or daughter expressed disappointment with gender roles or body parts? If a GNC child makes such a comment and the response is negative, the comment may never be repeated. But the child may continue to feel strongly that there is a mismatch between body and self.

For some parents of transgender teens the situation is not so clear. Perhaps their daughter was never a tomboy who hated wearing dresses, yet suddenly as a teen she is declaring she is really a boy. Or there is the son who seemed in no way different from other boys, yet now he says he is a girl inside. Life presents us with endless variations, including the existence of these individuals who seemed comfortable and acted in accordance with their assigned gender in childhood, but now feel strongly that their gender is different. If your child's disclosure of transgenderism seems to come out of the blue, then you will all need more time and discussion to gain a full understanding of her or his inner truth.

CHAPTER FOUR

# SEXUALITY AND GENDER

*Being transsexual doesn't have a whole lot to do with the act of sex, although I'm sure that there are some transpeople out there who are getting a whole lot luckier than I am.*

— Matt Kailey, *Just Add Hormones*

So far we've talked about biological sex and gender but not about sexuality: sexual attractions and sexual behavior. But as we all know, when we're talking about teens we can't leave out sexuality!

**Sexual orientation is not the same as gender**

At this point I want to clarify for you that sexual orientation (sexual attraction) is separate from gender identity and gender expression. Some people believe that transgender people are just confused gays or lesbians. Most parents would prefer to find out that their transgender kids are gay or lesbian, rather than trans-gender. While they face many challenges, gays and lesbians are accepted more easily in our society. The challenges of being trans-sexual are tougher. But just as a person does not choose to be gay or straight, one does not choose to be transgender or conventionally gendered.

Some transgender people do go through a phase of identifying themselves as gay or lesbian. They may already be viewed by others as gay or lesbian because of the stereotype that masculine women are lesbian and feminine men are gay. Before they have the understanding, language and courage to come out as transsexual, considering themselves to be gay or lesbian may seem to be the best fit. In this way, many transpeople go through the coming out process more than once. They initially accept society's judgment that if they are sexually attracted to people with the same body type then they must be homosexual. Their view changes as they learn about transgenderism and gain a new understanding of themselves.

**Spectrum of sexual orientations**

Once again, this is getting confusing, so let me explain it in more detail. Sexual orientation has to do with who we find attractive. Sexual orientation exists across a spectrum. (This was one of the important findings of Kinsey's study of sexuality in the US in the 1940s.) A man may be attracted to only women, mostly women, men and women, mostly men or only men. (And for some people, who may use the term "pansexual", gender is not a highly relevant factor in their sexual attractions.) So we can see there is a spectrum from heterosexual to bisexual to homosexual or, in today's language, straight to bi to gay.

If you are certain of your own gender, and aware of your attractions to males and females in varying degrees, you can find your place on this spectrum. Most people in our culture understand themselves to be gay, straight or bisexual, although not all pursue relationships precisely in accordance with their sexual orientation. Societal pressures steer us towards the heterosexual end of the spectrum, so many bisexuals as well as some lesbians and gays present themselves to others as straight. With increasing acceptance of homosexuality as a normal variation in human sexuality, this occurs less often.

## Putting it together: sexuality and gender

To illustrate these concepts, let's take a look at a transsexual person with a female body and a male gender identity who is attracted to females. If she, and others, understand her to be female, then she is a lesbian. Many female-to-male (FTM) transsexuals spend part of their lives being "out" as lesbian, part of the lesbian community, often fully accepted by friends and family as lesbian. But since the FTM individual truly feels himself to be male and is attracted to females, he is actually a heterosexual male in a female body. If he is able to transition (more about that later) to being male, he will be seen by others as the heterosexual male he is, and not as a lesbian. For him, being lesbian was only a transitional identity on his way to being a straight man.

Of course, some transsexuals are attracted to both genders and some to the initially "opposite" sex, so these folks are gay, lesbian or bisexual after transitioning. Here are two fictional examples to help you understand:

**Sam** was a quiet, artistic boy, quite different from his boisterous older sister. He loved drawing pictures of princesses and fairies. He thoroughly enjoyed dressing in his sister's clothes and imagining he was "Princess Samantha." Most of his playmates were girls. He occasionally told his parents he was really a girl. They took that as a sign of his vivid imagination.

Sam's parents allowed him to dress up at home, but drew the line when he wanted to wear a dress to school. They let him grow his hair long and never pressured him to play sports. They understood that he was different from the other boys and had trouble fitting in.

In middle school Sam was often teased for being feminine. He decided to cut his hair short and join the track team, so he could be one of the guys. The teasing stopped. Sam realized he was attracted to boys and began to think of himself as gay. At the same time, he didn't like his developing male body and felt more like a girl inside.

Sam now attends a support group for LGBT teens. No one there gives him a hard time about his femininity. He has started dating a gay boy he met there, but he has not told anyone at school that he is gay. When Sam thinks of his future, he imagines himself as a woman married to a man. We can understand Sam to be a heterosexual female in a male body. Being gay is just a transitional identity for Sam.

**Tiffany** grew up as a bright girl with varied interests. She enjoyed friendships with girls and boys. She loved to ski and played saxophone in the school band. She was happy and imagined a future of wide-open possibilities. Tiffany didn't think much about what was different or special about being a girl.

In puberty, Tiffany's developing breasts and hips didn't feel right to her. She was attracted to boys, but didn't like to be viewed as an attractive female. She no longer liked the feminine sound of her name. She cut her hair short and asked her friends to call her "T.J."

Now T.J. wears loose clothes to hide her female shape. When she looks in the mirror she is hoping to see a male body looking back at her. Searching online she found information about being transgender and realized it applied to her. Suddenly she had words to describe how she felt. She ordered a binder – a garment to safely flatten the breasts and create a more masculine appearance.

With her male gender identity and her attraction to boys, we can understand T.J. to be a gay boy in a girl's body. We can see her developing into an adult gay male.

I hope these two examples have helped you gain a better understanding of the relationship between sexual orientation and gender identity. It's not important that you sort this out all at once. Your teen will be sorting it out and, hopefully, explaining it to you. All you need to do is keep an open mind and be aware that the possibilities are quite wide ranging. It is helpful to understand that for most transgender people, having the opportunity to present oneself true to one's gender identity is of paramount importance. Concerns about the gender of a sex partner or finding a life mate are secondary. In fact, many transgender teens hold off on dating and intimacy until they are able to sort through and express their gender in a way that feels right for them.

# CHAPTER FIVE

# PUBERTY AND ADOLESCENCE

*The world's definitions are one thing and the life one actually lives is quite another.*

— James Baldwin, *The Evidence of Things Not Seen*

## Gender nonconforming teenagers

What happens to our strongly gender nonconforming kids when they start puberty? Teens who don't look and act like typical boys and girls are likely to bear the brunt of increased harassment. They are presumed to be gay or lesbian, and to the extent that anti-gay feelings are strong in their community, they suffer. For those who *are* lesbian or gay, there may be support from a Gay Straight Alliance at school, or an LGBT Community Center. There are inclusive images of gay and lesbian individuals and families in the mainstream media. Many lesbian and gay teenagers now have the full support of their families and friends.

But what about the kids who appear different and are actually transgender? To date, supports for these kids are absent in most communities. Families are rarely prepared to understand and accept their transgender youth. These kids are most often going through this process alone and in secret. Many are able to seek out information and support on the internet. Few have the in-person support and access to information that they truly need. They may be the only transgender teen present if they attend an LGBT youth group.

When transgender kids reach puberty, their bodies begin to betray them. They develop the physical characteristics that are typical of their biological sex but not in accord with their deeply felt gender. For example, boys see girls developing breasts and feel envious. Any growth of facial hair is disturbing. Girls are appalled when their breasts begin to develop. Menstruation is a monthly reminder of having the wrong body.

## Two strong indicators of transsexual experience

There are two strong indicators of transsexual experience. The first is the discomfort transsexual teens feel about the gendered aspects of their bodies, such as their genitals. The second is their desire to be perceived by others as belonging to the gender they feel they are. For some transsexual teens, significant distress about these matters doesn't begin until adolescence. But for all transsexual teens, the physical changes of puberty increase the distress. Puberty heightens the physical differences between the sexes. As the body's sexual characteristics become more glaringly obvious with each new development, the discordance with who they are inside becomes more and more disturbing. Comments from others about becoming a young man or a young woman only exacerbate this distress. In childhood, transgender individuals often maintained magical ideas about it all working out in the future. For transsexual teens in puberty, this no longer seems possible. As puberty progresses, many begin to feel hopeless about their future.

## Despair and isolation

Most transgender adolescents struggle with depression at some point. They may feel hopeless about ever being at ease with who they are. They may believe it is impossible to explain how they feel to their parents and friends. They are likely to fear that disbelief and disappointment will be the result if they choose to do so. They may fear they will lose friends if they share this secret, that word will spread and they will be shunned by all of their peers. Some transgender teens live with the fear that disclosure to family will lead to rejection, physical violence or homelessness.

Transgender teens come to dislike looking at themselves in the mirror. Each time they do, they are disappointed to see that their outer appearance does not fit with the girl or boy they feel themselves to be inside. They may adopt clothes or postures that hide their physical developments, or try to find unisex ways of presenting themselves as neither boy nor girl. They avoid public restrooms, where one has to declare one's gender to enter. They feel out of place in the restroom that coincides with their biology, and look out of place in the one that fits their gender identity. They often avoid pools and beaches where they have to display their body to others.

## Trying to fit in

Transgender teens who were consistently gender nonconforming in childhood may make an effort to conform to society's expectations, based on their biological sex, for some part of their teenage years. This gives them the ability to fit in with peers and get relief from criticism, taunting and the feeling that they are disappointing their parents. Generally, this effort to change one's outer self to please others leads to only a temporary sense of relief. For the child who is truly transgender, at some point the urge to be her or his authentic self will return full force. Pretending to be conventional will itself cause great distress. For this reason, transgender teens often exhibit mood swings over a period of months or years prior to their disclosure of their transgender identity.

## Mental health risks

As a result of these stresses, transgender teens are at risk of serious depression, suicide, self-harming behaviors, substance abuse and low self-esteem. The situation is worse for teens whose differences are not accepted by their families. Research has shown that transgender youths who are rejected by their families have lower self-esteem and are more isolated than youths whose families accept them.[1] They have poorer health and higher rates of depression, suicide, substance abuse problems and HIV infection than their peers who report having families and caregivers who support them. Even a little less rejection and a little more family acceptance increases self-esteem, access to social support and life satisfaction, while decreasing the rate of problems. Chapter 7 will explain how best to support and nurture your transgender teen.

As I mentioned above, a teenager's silent inner struggle with gender identity can lead to mood swings. Sometimes the mood swings are viewed by parents and others as typical adolescent emotionality and behavior. When the mood swings persist, the teen may be sent for counseling and/or psychiatric medication. These treatments are largely ineffective if a significant piece of information (the child's gender identity struggle) is missing. The teen's condition will be worse if there is disrespect and harassment due to gender nonconformance. A teen's condition will be most severe if he or she feels rejected by the family.

Let's look at the story of a transgender teenager who became depressed. While this is a fictional example, it reflects the real-life experience of many of my transgender teen clients.

**Cassie** was an athletic girl. She enjoyed playing football with her older brother and his friends. She had little interest in spending time with other girls in the neighborhood. When she joined a girls' soccer team, she soon became a star player. She was a good student, with an easygoing personality.

As they grew older, Cassie's brother and his friends no longer included her in their games. Cassie's feelings were hurt. Her mother explained to her that her brother

---

[1] "Supportive Families, Healthy Children: Helping Families with Lesbian, Gay, Bisexual and Transgender Children," Caitlin Ryan, PhD, Family Acceptance Project, 2009.

was getting older and it was natural that he didn't want his little sister tagging along anymore. Her mom said she shouldn't take it personally. Cassie's brother was still nice to her at other times, but she couldn't help feeling sad and left out.

At school Cassie hung out with her friends from the soccer team. In middle school these girls became more interested in clothes, wearing makeup, and talking about boys. Cassie was interested in none of these things. She began to feel that she didn't fit in anywhere. Cassie's mother sensed that Cassie was at an awkward stage. She talked to Cassie about how exciting it could be to become a young woman. She offered to spend some "girl" time together. They could go shopping or do their nails. She would show Cassie how to put on makeup. Cassie refused. Cassie's father wondered if they had made a mistake allowing her to spend so much time with her brother and his friends when she was younger. He told his wife they should have set up more play dates with girls.

Cassie still enjoyed soccer, but she felt sad and angry at home and at school. Her grades declined. Her friends found her to be moody. To her parents it seemed that their easygoing daughter had suddenly become angry and uncooperative. Some days she refused to go to school. Cassie didn't understand why she felt so bad. She hated feeling miserable. She didn't want to upset her parents and her friends.

A guidance counselor recommended a therapist for Cassie. In therapy, Cassie began to talk about feeling out of place. She didn't fit in with the girls and wasn't included by the boys. She felt her parents were disappointed in her and her friends didn't like her anymore.

When she felt more comfortable with her therapist, Cassie revealed that she often imagined herself as a boy named Marcus. In this fantasy Marcus was the captain of the football team. He was dating a popular girl at school. Cassie never imagined herself as anyone's girlfriend. In fact, she hated the idea of becoming a young woman.

Cassie's therapist had recently attended a conference about LGBT youth. She understood that it was important for Cassie to be free of others' expectations as she explored her identity. Feeling supported in therapy, Cassie became less angry and moody at home and at school.

As Cassie learned about gay, lesbian, bisexual and transgender identities, she realized she was transgender. Understanding this helped her feel less confused and less alone. She found that once she understood and accepted herself, she got along better with her friends and her family. Her grades began to improve.

Cassie's parents were pleased with the changes in her mood. They were interested to learn what had been troubling her and what had helped her feel better. When Casssie told her parents she was transgender, they had trouble believing it at first. When they considered how much better she was feeling since coming to this realization, they tried to be open-minded about it. Thinking back on her childhood, they recognized that she had always behaved more like a boy than a girl. This helped them accept that perhaps Cassie's true identity was male.

As in this story, once the child's gender identity is understood and respected, the mental health condition generally improves. In many cases, depression virtually disappears once a teen is feeling fully supported. For this reason, it is extremely important that any mental health assessment and treatment of a gender nonconforming child or teen be provided by a clinician knowledgeable about LGBT youth. See Chapters 8 and 9 for information on finding a counselor who is a gender identity therapist.

CHAPTER SIX

# BALANCING AUTHENTICITY AND SAFETY

*It's necessary that I no longer live as a female. Necessary for my mental survival, if not actually great for my day-to-day physical life.*
— Ellen Wittlinger, *Parrotfish*

## Authenticity

Adolescence is a time to figure out who you are. For teens who have realized that their gender identity and their bodies don't match, being authentically themselves becomes of paramount importance. Their distress about the difference between who they feel they are inside and who they appear to be on the outside increases. They feel stung when others refer to them as the boy or girl they appear to be, rather than who they feel they are inside. They assume, often correctly, that those who care most about them will not be able to accept this aspect of who they really are. They struggle with telling others, perhaps hinting about it at first. They may try out a public identity of lesbian or gay to see how much others can understand and accept.

A teenager who has broken through the fear of disclosure, and has begun to tell parents about being transgender, will often be extremely impatient about making a transition. Transsexual teens may feel they have been suffering for years, forced to live in the wrong gender role. They cannot understand how difficult it is for parents to come to view a daughter as a son, or to accept a son who suddenly wants to live as a female.

Transsexual teens often feel completely certain of their gender identity, and have little or no fear about taking hormones or having surgery. Parents have tremendous fears and concerns. Most often, transsexual teens are advocating for immediate full authenticity, while parents advocate for caution and safety, putting the two parties at odds. Let's look at what some of your fears and concerns are likely to be if you are the parent of a transsexual teen requesting social transition (living full time in the new gender), hormones and (eventually as an adult) surgery.

## Confront Your Fears

### Fear of harassment

Perhaps your child has already experienced harassment from peers for being gender nonconforming. As a parent, you expect this will only worsen if your child announces at school that he is a girl from now on, or she is a boy. Of the teens I have worked with (primarily students of public and private high schools in Connecticut), most have not experienced increased harassment when they made a social transition at school. It helped when the student made the social transition with certainty and confidence. If the student can seem at ease about it, others are likely to be more accepting. The student's more open-minded peers will lead the way by treating the teen who has transitioned as just one of the guys, or girls. See Chapters 8 and 9 for more about the social transition at school.

## Fear of physical harm

We have all by now heard of tragic incidents in which transgender teens and adults are attacked or killed. Parents worry especially about violence from schoolmates. For this reason, the social transition at school includes meeting with school administration. Steps are taken to establish a safe and respectful environment for your child at school. If you do not come to feel that your child can be safe at his or her school, you will look for a safe alternative.

As adults involved in the care of transgender teens, we must help them establish as much safety as possible. We must also realize that teens who are not allowed to transition are at increased risk of depression, substance abuse, self-loathing, self-harm or suicide, so refusing the teen's request outright is also a dangerous path. We must work to spread the idea that being transgender is a normal variation in gender identity. This will help over time reduce prejudice and violence against transgender people.

## Fear of regret

Parents fear that their teen will have a change of mind after it's too late. They fear that later on in life, he or she will feel that taking hormones was a mistake. But experience shows that teens who feel strongly that they are transsexual are highly likely to continue feeling that way in adulthood.[2] Before starting hormones there will be a period of psychotherapy and most likely a social transition. This will allow time for the teen, the parents and those evaluating the teen to be confident before any permanent medical intervention begins.

When it comes to teenagers under the age of 16, only fully reversible hormonal interventions will be considered. These are hormones that postpone puberty but do not eliminate the option of subsequently going through puberty in accordance with the

---

[2] "Medical Care for Gender Variant Young People: Dealing with the Practical Problems," B.W. Reed, P.T. Cohen-Kettinis, T. Reed, and N. Spack, *Sexologies*, 17:4, October – December 2008, pp. 258-264.

biological birth sex. Cross gender hormones (for a transition to the other biological sex) will not be considered generally until the teen is 16 or 17 years old and has had adequate time to attain certainty about the wish to transition. (See Chapters 8 and 9 for more information about interventions.)

It is also helpful to know that research has shown there is a very low rate of regret among adults who have made a full medical transition.[3] The regrets that do occur are mostly related to poor surgical outcomes, or rejection by family or society. This tells us that the vast majority of the individuals in these studies remained consistent in their belief that their affirmed gender identity is the right one for them.

## Examine Your Concerns

### Too young

"My child is too young to be certain about something this serious": Parents often recall ideas and interests they had as teens that they no longer hold. They imagine gender identity to be similar to ideas about career, or raising a family, ideas that generally do change as we mature into young adults (and often throughout our adulthood.) Gender identity is more viscerally felt, and more intrinsic to oneself. As a result we can attain a high level of certainty about a teen's gender identity through the process of psychotherapy and through the experience gained from a social transition.

The therapist examines the development of gender identity in childhood. Parents provide the therapist with their view of their child's feelings and behaviors at various ages. Teens talk in therapy sessions about their comfort and their struggles through

---

[3] "Eligibility and Readiness for Sex Reassignment Surgery: Recommendations for Revision of the WPATH *Standards of Care*," Griet de Cuypere and Herman Vercruysse, Jr., *International Journal of Transgenderism*, 11:3, July – September 2009, pp. 194-205.

many aspects of growing up. Therapy gives teens an opportunity to speak at length about their sense of self. They discuss in detail their feelings and behaviors related to gender identity. The therapist observes whether the two strong indicators of transsexual experience are present: discomfort with the gendered aspects of their bodies, and a desire to be perceived by others as belonging to the gender they feel inside. The therapist then monitors the teen's certainty about these feelings over time, including the time of the social transition.

## Not really transgender

"My child is not trangender but is saying so for one of the following reasons":

- Mental illness.
- As an emotional reaction to a life trauma or circumstance.
- To be rebellious.
- To get attention.
- To fit in with countercultural friends.

While any of these explanations may be true in rare cases, generally teens who say they are transgender are transgender, in the general all-inclusive sense of the word. Evaluation by a gender identity therapist (a mental health clinician specializing in gender identity) will clarify those instances in which the child is suffering from a delusion, or lying about gender to gain attention, fit in, or upset parents. These teens' description of their gender identity and their responses to questions from a knowledgeable professional will not be consistent with what we know to be true of transgender individuals. In particular, a gender identity therapist can help a young person clarify whether or not he or she is transsexual. Being transsexual is the only circumstance leading eventually to irreversible interventions. The child who starts out saying she is transsexual but ends up realizing rather that she is genderfluid, for example, will continue to explore this aspect of her identity through young adulthood and will not need any major interventions as a teen.

## No need to transition

"Nowadays a girl can do anything a boy can do and vice versa": Being transsexual is not about gaining access to certain activities or jobs. Transsexuals have a deeply felt need to be seen by others as being of the gender they feel inside, and a deeply felt discomfort with the gendered aspects of the body they were born with. It can be difficult for parents and other concerned individuals to grasp what this means, as it is an experience unfamiliar to conventionally gendered individuals (those whose biological sex is the same as their gender identity.) It will be important for you to listen closely as your teen explains this important aspect of his or her inner experience.

## Your own discomfort

Parents are generally uncomfortable with the idea of transgender. Most parents do not know anyone who is transgender and initially react to the child's disclosure with tremendous discomfort. Parents may have been taught that being transsexual is a sickness, immoral, or perverted. It is extremely important as the parent of a transgender child to get free of these negative beliefs. You must educate yourself about the variety of gender identities that exist and open yourself to a full understanding of what is natural and true for your child.

## The reactions of others

"What will others think?" (Friends, colleagues, community, extended family): Parents worry about how others will react to the news that their child is transgender, and what others will think of them for having a transgender child. These worries are natural and understandable. But you must not let them get in the way of supporting your transgender child and making decisions in the best interest of your child. Most parents inform only a small number of close friends or family members at first, while the child's gender identity is being discussed and considered. Once a decision has been made for a social transition, parents can consider various options for informing others in person, by phone, by letter or email. It is important to present this new information in a positive light. Explain that you and your child have come to realize something essential about his or her identity. Request that others adopt the new name, corresponding pronouns, and a respectful manner. (This topic is addressed in more detail in Chapters 8 and 9.)

When you speak to friends and family, it is important to acknowledge their discomfort and let them know if you felt the same way at first. Tell them that you welcome a chance to respond to any questions or concerns they have about your child's transition. Ask for their acceptance and support. You will see, if you have not already, that you are making a major transition as well when your child transitions.

**Feelings of loss**

By the time your child has reached adolescence, you have come to enjoy this boy or girl as someone with a stable gender. Some of your appreciation of your child is connected to your own feelings and assumptions about what it means for the child to be female or male, and what the future holds in store. Despite the notion that we live in a culture where anyone can do anything, regardless of gender, we carry many differing expectations for men and women. These ideas deeply affect our views of who our children are and who they may become. So parents may experience a deep sense of loss when they discover that a child will be changing in outward appearance and identity to conform to a long-felt but previously secret alternative gender identity. It is important for you to have as much time as you need to feel and accept the loss. Talk it over with your spouse or partner, close friends and family, or a mental health professional. It is helpful to let your child know about your feelings of loss, so your teen can understand the ways in which this is a difficult adjustment for you, but it is best not to dwell on this with her or him. It is not your child's job to help you with this loss. Other supportive adults can do that for you.

## Coming to Terms with These Fears and Concerns

Pay attention to all of these possible fears and concerns. It is important to address each one that affects you. This will help you prepare to be the best support you can be for your child at this challenging time for all of you. The next chapter will discuss ways to nurture your child at this important juncture in your lives.

CHAPTER SEVEN

# NURTURING YOUR TRANSGENDER TEEN

*MAMI (to PAPI): When I was pregnant, we didn't care what we were having, we just wanted a healthy, happy baby. So if we loved her then, before we knew she was a girl, why can't we love her now, as a boy?*
— Janis Astor del Valle, *Becoming Joaquin*

**Keep an open mind**

The most helpful thing you can do for your transgender child is to adopt an open-minded attitude toward whatever your child is saying about gender identity and gender expression. Don't be afraid to ask questions. Recognize that it is natural for parents, because of the fears and concerns discussed in Chapter 6, to have a bias against believing that a child may be transsexual. This will be especially true if your child's behavior until now has been relatively in keeping with society's gender expectations. Accepting that a child is transsexual is easier for parents when the child grew up as strongly gender nonconforming. Remember that if your first response is to strongly oppose what your teen is saying about gender identity, he or she is more likely to adopt a stubborn, oppositional point of view in future discussions

## Keep the lines of communication open

A teen who feels you are listening will continue to talk to you. Supportive interaction with your transgender teen reduces the risk of low self-esteem, depression and suicide. It increases the likelihood that your child will let you know of any self-harm or substance abuse. (If your teen is engaging in dangerous behavior, seek professional help.) Stay as fully engaged as you can with your teen. While teenagers typically pull away from their parents and relate more closely with their peers, transgender teens need their parents' active support.

## What did I do wrong?

Many parents wonder if they did something wrong in raising their child who turned out to be transgender. Should I have kept him from playing with dolls and encouraged more rough and tumble activities? Should I have been less enthusiastic about her being such a tomboy? Did I secretly wish she would be a boy because I already had two daughters? Did this happen because there weren't adult men in his life after his father was gone?

You didn't do anything to cause your child to be transgender! How we interact with our children does not determine their gender identity. Our interactions *do* have an effect on their self-esteem, so it's important to let them know we accept them as they are. You may have made the mistake of criticizing or shaming your child for gender nonconforming behaviors. You may have done so out of fear or ignorance. Now is your opportunity to correct that mistake by expressing your love and support, even when your child's behavior makes you uncomfortable.

## Handle your own discomfort

Most parents are uncomfortable when their teens choose to act or dress in keeping with their transgender identity. It is important to handle your own discomfort. Do not pressure your child to act or dress conventionally for your comfort. Learn to appreciate your teen's uniqueness and courage. This will help you get over any feelings of shame or embarrassment. When transgender teens are harassed for their unconventional ways, it is essential for parents to respond with full support. Don't blame your teen for the harassment. All people deserve to live a fully authentic life. If others respond badly, that is not your teen's fault. Your role as a parent is to see what can be done to eliminate or reduce the harassment without sacrificing your child's right to be self-affirming.

**When your teen has doubts**

Even those teens who at times feel certain they are transsexual will at other times have some doubts about it. This is not surprising, given society's negative attitudes about transgender people. It is difficult to embrace an identity that feels correct for oneself but is considered abnormal or pathological by others. There may have been a time early in life when your son told someone he trusts that "I'm really a girl" or "I have the wrong body," and he was gently (or harshly) told "No, you're a boy." Perhaps it was explained to him that having a penis indicates decisively that he is a boy and not a girl. Those responses, even though well-intentioned, send an early message that it's not acceptable to be (or consider or talk about being) transgender. As a result, it's difficult for transgender teens to be confident that what they know and feel inside is real. Some teens respond to this lack of confidence by adopting a rigid and demanding stance about transitioning. Some are plagued with self-doubt. Transgender teens need to feel supported in their exploration, without prejudgment. The must be free to try out whatever types of gender expression and identity feel comfortable and correct for them.

**Mixed messages**

While it is your role as a parent to raise safety concerns, you have to be quite careful about the mixed message in statements such as "It's okay to crossdress at home but not at school." Often, transgender teens feel the need to try out authentic gender expression in public even if there may be a hostile response from peers and others. These teens are no longer willing to suppress their true selves for the sake of fitting in and being liked and getting treated better by others. It is important to recognize that the challenges, in our culture, for a boy who wishes to go to school dressed as a girl are more substantial than those for a girl who goes to school as a boy. Parents must work with the school and the community for this to be a safe and respected step for your child to take. This is better than simply accepting the belief that societal prejudice makes it too risky to proceed.

**Learn from your own experiences**

In your own life, did you honor and disclose something about yourself that others may have criticized or condemned? Did you keep an important part of your identity or desires secret in order to have others' approval? We can all recall facing this kind of dilemma at some point in our lives. Most of us find out that in the long run it is better to be true to ourselves and worry less about the responses of others. This is an especially tough challenge for teenagers, whether it's about clothes, music, unpopular interests or friends, sexuality, or gender identity and expression. We must do our best to support teens who are grappling with issues of authenticity, integrity, and societal disapproval. As the parent of a transgender teen, you must put aside, as best you can, your discomfort with your child's gender identity or unconventional gender expression.

**Support your child**

These tips will help you be supportive at this challenging time. (To get started locating resources, contact an LGBT Community Center or see Chapter 11 of this book.):

- Whenever possible, transgender teens need the company and support of other transgender teens and adults. Find out if there is a support group that your teen can join.

- Attend a support group for parents, or seek out an online parents' group.

- Go with your child to an LGBT youth conference, even if this requires some travel.

- Explore safe online support networks for LGBT teens.

- When your child meets other transgender teenagers, encourage them to keep in touch. Welcome these friends to visit in your home. Support them spending time together in ordinary teenage activities, even if this makes you a little uneasy. You'll get used to it! And your child will be much better off when you do. These friends' parents can be an additional support for you.

**The next two chapters**

In the next two chapters we will look at the steps you can take when your child has told you he or she is transgender. To make things simpler I have written one chapter for the parents of a male-bodied teen who feels she is a girl (Chapter 8) and a separate chapter for the parents of a female-bodied teen who feels he is a boy (Chapter 9). They cover much the same ground so there is no need to read both.

# CHAPTER EIGHT

# TAKING STEPS: MALE TO FEMALE

*Courage is more exhilarating than fear and in the long run it is easier. We do not have to become heroes overnight. Just a step at a time, meeting each thing that comes up, seeing it not as dreadful as it appeared, discovering we have the strength to stare it down.*

*– Eleanor Roosevelt, You Learn by Living*

## Knowledge and Understanding

Your first step is to learn as much as you can about your child's gender identity and about transgender people in general. You must address each of the challenges you face when you contemplate that your child may be transgender, including any of those discussed in Chapter 6. Then listen with an open mind and an open heart to what he has to say about his own experience, his sense of his gender, and how he would like to proceed if he feels he is really a girl. Read as much as you can about being transgender, keeping in mind that your son's experience is unique. There is not only one typical life path for a transgender person. Look for any organizations, conferences or support groups in your area for transgender individuals and their families. See the resource list in Chapter 11 for books, organizations and websites.

# Counseling

A mental health professional who is knowledgeable about gender identity can be an enormous help to your child and your family. This gender identity therapist will be able to help you and your child sort out the nature of his gender identity. Counseling will help you come to terms with any discomfort you have if your child is transgender so you can offer him the full support he needs. The gender identity therapist will also be able to help you decide about and navigate through any additional steps your child wants to take, especially if he is transsexual. This will include referrals to local support groups, organizations and other health care providers, as well as suggestions about readings and information about any conferences in your area for transgender teens and their parents.

A gender identity therapist will be familiar with the World Professional Association for Transgender Health Standards of Care (formerly called the Harry Benjamin Standards of Care.) The Standards of Care are the most widely accepted guidelines for the use of hormones or surgery for transsexuals. One of the roles of this mental health clinician is to evaluate your teen's readiness for social transition, hormones or surgery. The gender identity therapist will explain to you and your teen the possible benefits and risks of each step. Benefits and risks of medical treatments will be discussed in more detail with the medical provider. You can view the Standards of Care at *www.wpath.org.*

These web sites may help you find a therapist in your area who is experienced in the treatment of transgender persons:

- Dr. Becky Allison: *www.drbecky.com/therapists.html.*

- Laura's Playground:
  *www.laurasplayground.com/gender_therapists.htm*

- The World Professional Association for Transgender Health *www.wpath.org.* From the home page click on "find a provider" then just enter your State (if you are in the U.S.) and click on "submit."

If possible, it is best to verify independently that the therapist you find is fully credentialed and licensed. You can do this by speaking with a local health care provider.

## Social Transition

If you and your child have come to agree that he is transsexual (a female in a male body) or most likely transsexual, the next important and useful step is to allow him to make a social transition to female. This is the point at which you will begin using female pronouns when you refer to your teen. You will do your best to call him by his preferred female name. For parents this is a difficult adjustment, from a practical standpoint, given the years of calling your child by his male name and thinking of him as your son. And of course it is difficult from an emotional standpoint as well if you remain troubled or uncertain about your child's new gender identity.

A social transition means your biologically male child who identifies as a girl will choose a moment to begin presenting himself in public as a girl. At first this may be limited to only at school, or in some other specific context, but eventually the social transition is full time. You will be ready to endorse this transition when you:

- feel fairly certain that your child should take this step to find out if his sense of his female gender is authentic, or

- are aware that your child is in great distress over having to be considered male and you would like to give him the opportunity to experience some relief.

For most transsexual teens, the primary challenges for social transition are at school and at extended family gatherings. One key indicator of readiness for a social transition is the child's sense that the relief from being true to himself will outweigh any harassment he may encounter. It is difficult to know in advance the amount of harassment your teen may experience. Many parents expect harassment to increase when a teenager makes a social transition. In my experience, however, many kids who had been harassed earlier for being gender nonconforming were treated better once they became confident about making the social transition. An increasingly androgynous presentation (long hair, jewelry, make-up, feminine clothes) by the teen prior to the transition will give you some ability to anticipate the likely level of harassment and plan accordingly.

**Making the social transition at school**

The following steps have helped my clients accomplish the social transition more smoothly:

- Your teen will begin by informing close friends that he is a girl. He will gradually dress in a more androgynous manner if he has not already done so. He will find that friends who have already shown themselves to be accepting of gays, lesbians, and gender nonconforming people are likely to be most supportive. If your teen had previously come out as a gay male, he will already know which of his peers are open-minded regarding these matters. (As mentioned in Chapter 4, some transgender people go through a phase of identifying as gay or lesbian.)

- Next, you and your teen will meet with school administrators (or perhaps first with a sympathetic teacher or guidance counselor) to request the transition. If there is a GSA (Gay Straight Alliance) or similar LGBT support organization at your child's school, the group's advisor is a good person to contact first. You and your child will explain that he is transsexual. You may have to explain to administrators what that means. You will request that he be viewed as female at school and addressed by his chosen female name and female pronouns.

- You will request that the school take whatever steps it deems necessary to assure more open-mindedness about gender diversity (such as presentations for students and/or faculty by a diversity advocacy group) and to guarantee, to the greatest extent possible, that you child is safe at school and will be treated with respect. If your school administration's response is unsatisfactory, a good resource to call on is Trans Youth Family Allies (*www.imatyfa.org*). Any LGBT youth organizations in your region, such as the wonderful True Colors, in Connecticut (*www.ourtruecolors.org*), can provide valuable assistance. It is the school administration's responsibility to assure that teachers and students will be educated about gender diversity, that teachers will honor the student's gender identity and that harassment will not be tolerated.

- The school will need to identify a bathroom for the teen to use (usually a single bathroom such as in the nurse's office) and make provisions for changing and showering for gym class or sports.

- Generally, word of mouth along with your teen's answers to any friendly questions about his female presentation will suffice to orient the rest of the student body to the new gender.

While this process has worked repeatedly for the teens who have been my clients, it is important to discuss with your teen what approach would make him most comfortable. You should discuss with the school administration (with sympathetic staff included in the discussion) what steps they believe will achieve the smoothest transition. Then get ready to take it in stride when your son's friends call, asking for him by his female name, or teachers tell you what a pleasure it is to have *her* in their class.

You may discover that school personnel have many of the same fears and concerns you and other parents have experienced (see Chapter 6). Be patient and persistent in encouraging them to address these fears and concerns. Ask them to keep in mind that your child's welfare depends on his ability to make the social transition. If you encounter extreme hostility at any point in this process, you and your child may also decide that alternate schooling is the best and safest choice. It will not be best for your son to abandon his need to be his authentic female self if that path becomes more difficult. If that should happen, just pull back, reassess your options, and find another way to move forward.

## Informing family and friends

Telling the extended family and friends of the family is a stressful experience for most parents of transsexual teens. Fear of rejection and criticism, or fear of causing unmanageable distress for older family members is common. Many families keep this matter secret until a family or social gathering is coming. My recommendation to teens is that they defer to their parents, whenever possible, on notifying the relatives and adult family friends. My recommendation to parents is that they begin early on disclosing to close friends and family that their son is questioning his gender identity. This lays the groundwork for a later disclosure of the new female identity. As with your teen's disclosures, you will get the best responses from those who have already indicated in some way that they are open minded about LGBT people. Start with them first.

When it comes time for your child's social transition, it is important that you be in charge of how this information is shared with the extended family. In my experience, families have accomplished this by direct phone calls to each individual if the network is not that large, or by a letter or email if calling everyone is unmanageable. I do not recommend taking the short cut of asking one person to tell another, unless the intermediary knows your child well and is well-versed in information about transsexuals.

By the time you are ready to send this letter, you will have gained some comfort and consistency in using your child's female name and using female pronouns. This will be reflected in the way you write your letter. Notice that I use female pronouns in the following suggestions for the letter to extended family and friends. I will continue to use female pronouns, and also refer to your teen as your daughter, for the remainder of this chapter. Hopefully you will find this helpful, rather than confusing, as you continue to ponder what it means for your child to be transgender.

You may want to include some or all of the following points in your letter:

- Tell family and friends that you would like them to receive some important news about your teen with an open mind. Let them know as simply and clearly as you can that you have learned something new about your child's identity. Share the new name and ask that they be respectful and make every effort to use this name and female pronouns when they speak to or about your child.

- Explain that while your child's new gender was difficult for you to accept at first, you now know that this transition is best for your teen and will lead to the happiest outcome for her and for the family. You may add that this is something she has struggled with for a long time in silence. You are proud of her courage and glad she is finally able to be true to herself.

- Stress that she is the same person she was when they knew her as a boy, with all of the same positive attributes you all value and love. (Don't hesitate to mention what those wonderful characteristics are!)

- Let them know that you welcome any questions they have about this change and that you look forward to telling them more about this if they would like to know more. You can also recommend this book to them so they can become more familiar with what it means to be transgender.

Be sure to review the letter with your teen before you send it out so she is comfortable with what you have written. Your teen may want to send a separate letter, or include a personal message in yours.

Here, as an example, is the letter sent by Sam's parents. (See Sam's story in Chapter 4):

Dear Family and Friends,

We are writing to share some news about our son, Sam. Over the last few years, Sam has been thinking a lot about who he really is, deep down inside. Last year Sam bravely told us that he feels he is a girl in a boy's body. As you can imagine, we were upset to hear this and didn't really understand. While Sam has always enjoyed feminine activities, we just accepted him as different from other boys. We knew he was a free spirit, a gentle and imaginative child. We never considered that he might not feel that he is a boy.

Well, now we *do* understand. We'd like to help you understand and support Sam as he embarks on the challenging journey of becoming Samantha. Sam has been going to school as Samantha. We've been very pleased with the response from teachers and classmates. We are getting used to friends calling the house and asking for "Samantha." We can see how happy and comfortable our child is now that she is living as a girl. This has helped us feel good about supporting her transition to female in any way we can.

We know many challenges lie ahead for Samantha and for us. We ask you to approach this news with an open mind. Samantha would like you to use her new name from now on and to refer to her as "she." We have gradually learned to do so, although we occasionally slip up. This is a work-in-progress for all of us. Please continue to cherish and support her just as you did when she was a boy.

We are sending out this letter to get the discussion started. We look forward to having a chance to speak to you directly and answer any questions you may have.

Sincerely,

(For another example, see Chapter 9 for the letter sent by Cassie's parents. Cassie's story is in Chapter 5.)

### Other steps in the social transition

Along with changing name, pronouns, clothes and grooming, a transgirl who is well into male puberty may want to shave her body hair as well as any facial hair. As she becomes more certain that she is transsexual and heading for female adulthood, she may also want to consider electrolysis or laser treatment for permanent removal of facial or body hair. A transsexual youth may request a legal name change when she feels certain of her intent to make a full and permanent transition. This can generally be accomplished through your local probate court. If your child has made a social transition and legal name change, your gender identity therapist can help provide documentation, per your state's regulations, to have the gender marker on her driver's license changed to female. Having identification that is consistent with her gender presentation helps protect your teenager from harassment and keeps her transgender status private.

# Hormones

There are two types of hormonal treatments that can be offered to teenagers: puberty-blocking hormones and cross-gender hormones.

**Puberty-blocking hormones**

Puberty-blocking hormones are given to teens in the early stages of puberty who have met the following criteria:

- They have been gender nonconforming since childhood,
- They have completed 6 months of psychotherapy, and
- They have already made a social transition or feel that they are likely to want to do so.

These hormones suspend the bodily changes of puberty, giving the teen more time to decide on a future course. If by age 16 or 17 your biologically male teen who has been taking puberty-blocking hormones determines that her gender is female, she can initiate cross-gender hormones with a better physical (female) outcome than if she had gone through male puberty before transitioning. She will be less likely to need facial feminization surgery as an adult to pass well as female. If, however, your teen concludes that he is *not* transsexual, the puberty-blocking hormones are discontinued and he will experience a delayed but otherwise normal male puberty.

**Cross-gender hormones**

Cross-gender hormones are the second category of hormones. These can be given to teens as young as 16 years old, according to the Standards of Care. These hormones (primarily estrogen for male-to-female) allow the body to conform more closely to the individual's gender identity. Many transsexual teens feel some emotional relief immediately upon starting to take hormones, although the desired physical changes (breasts, fuller hips and softer skin for MTF) will take some months to begin and a number of years to reach completion. Taking cross-gender hormones creates certain medical risks and may lead to infertility. These are matters which the teen and her parents must discuss with the gender identity therapist before a referral is made to an endocrinologist knowledgeable about cross-gender hormones. These concerns will be discussed further with the endocrinologist and relevant lab tests will be done before your teen can start taking hormones.

Your daughter will have to take cross-gender hormones throughout her life if she wants all of the changes caused by the hormones to persist. The medical risks will also persist as long as she is taking hormones. Therefore it is essential that your daughter maintains regular visits with the endocrinologist and completes all lab tests as requested to maintain the highest level of medical safety. It is important to take the prescribed dose exactly as directed by the doctor. It is not safe to seek hormones without a doctor's prescription. Electrolysis or laser hair removal can be considered for MTF teens with significant facial or body hair, along with or prior to taking cross-gender hormones. Your child's gender identity therapist will help you and your teen think through the hormone options, clarify when hormone treatment may be indicated, and make a referral to an appropriate physician at your request.

**Impatient teens**

Many transgender teens are exceedingly anxious to begin taking hormones, long before their parents have enough information to consider such a request, or the confidence that such intervention is right for their child. You will have to ask your teen to be patient as you take the time you need to understand her identity, her needs, and the realities of hormonal intervention. In most cases, a 3 or 6 month delay in starting hormones will not make an appreciable difference in long term outcome. (Exceptions to this would be a child experiencing rapid onset of puberty, or a teen who wants to start hormones during her senior year of high school to be able to pass better as female when she starts college.) I often point out to impatient teens that they are well ahead of the pack in that they have reached a clear understanding of their gender discordance and have parents who are engaged in this process with them. Most transsexuals have had to wait well into adulthood to have the understanding and resources to transition, and many have done so without any support or acceptance from their families.

# Surgery

Surgery for the purpose of having one's body conform to one's gender identity is not done prior to the age of 18. If your teen is requesting surgery, she will generally need your agreement and support (financial and otherwise) if she is to have surgery done in young adulthood. The most common surgeries sought by MTFs are facial feminization, Adam's apple reduction and genital surgery. For parents, the idea of genital surgery can be quite disturbing, even if it is something your child deeply desires. It is important to take the time you need to understand that your daughter is extremely uncomfortable about having male genitals. While your teen may look forward to the prospect of surgery, you may need time to grieve the loss of a cherished son. Keep in mind that for a long time she has not felt that she is a son. When you are ready, she needs to be cherished as your daughter. Most of the things you value and admire about her will be unchanged. She is likely after surgery to be happier and more at ease, more comfortable in her body.

These surgeries are steps which your young person is likely to take only after she is well into young adulthood, so your role as a parent in the process may be quite different at that point.

# CHAPTER NINE

# TAKING STEPS: FEMALE TO MALE

*Each of us deserves the freedom to pursue our own version of happiness; to make the most of our talents; to speak our minds; to not fit in; most of all, to be true to ourselves. That's the freedom that enriches all of us.*
   – Barack Obama, for the "It Gets Better" Project, whitehouse.gov

## Knowledge and Understanding

Your first step is to learn as much as you can about your child's gender identity and about transgender people in general. You must address each of the challenges you face when you contemplate that your child may be transgender, including any of those discussed in Chapter 6. Then listen with an open mind and an open heart to what she has to say about her own experience, her sense of her gender, and how she would like to proceed if she feels she is really a boy. Read as much as you can about being transgender, keeping in mind that your daughter's experience is unique. There is not only one typical life path for a transgender person. Look for any organizations, conferences or support groups in your area for transgender individuals and their families. See the resource listing in Chapter 11 for books, organizations and websites.

# Counseling

A mental health professional who is knowledgeable about gender identity can be an enormous help to your child and your family. This gender identity therapist will be able to help you and your child sort out the nature of her gender identity. Counseling will help you come to terms with any discomfort you have if your child is transgender so you can offer her the full support she needs. The gender identity therapist will also be able to help you decide about and navigate through any additional steps your child wants to take, especially if she is transsexual. This will include referrals to local support groups, organizations and other health care providers, as well as suggestions about readings and information about any conferences in your area for transgender teens and their parents.

A gender identity therapist will be familiar with the World Professional Association for Transgender Health Standards of Care (formerly called the Harry Benjamin Standards of Care.) The Standards of Care are the most widely accepted guidelines for the use of hormones or surgery for transsexuals. One of the roles of this mental health clinician is to evaluate your teen's readiness for social transition, hormones or surgery. The gender identity therapist will explain to you and your teen the possible benefits and risks of each step. Benefits and risks of medical treatments will be discussed in more detail with the medical provider. You can view the Standards of Care at *www.wpath.org.*

These web sites may help you find a therapist in your area who is experienced in the treatment of transgender persons:

• Dr. Becky Allison: *www.drbecky.com/therapists.html.*

- Laura's Playground:
  *www.laurasplayground.com/gender_therapists.htm*

- The World Professional Association for Transgender Health *www.wpath.org.* From the home page click on "find a provider" then just enter your State (if you are in the U.S.) and click on "submit."

If possible, it is best to verify independently that the therapist you find is fully credentialed and licensed. You can do this by speaking with a local health care provider.

## Social Transition

If you and your child have come to agree that she is transsexual (a male in a female body) or most likely transsexual, the next important and useful step is to allow her to make a social transition to male. This is the point at which you will make a shift and begin using male pronouns when you refer to your teen. You will make every effort to call her by her preferred male name. For parents this is a difficult adjustment, from a practical standpoint, given the years of calling your child by her female name and thinking of her as your daughter. And of course it is difficult from an emotional standpoint as well if you remain troubled or uncertain about your child's new gender identity.

A social transition means your biologically female child who identifies as a boy will choose a moment to begin presenting herself in public as a boy. At first this may be limited to only at school, or in some other specific context, but eventually the social transition is full time. You will be ready to endorse this transition when you:

- feel fairly certain that your child should take this step to find out if her sense of her male gender is authentic, or

- are aware that your child is in great distress over having to be considered female and you would like to give her the opportunity to experience some relief.

For most transsexual teens, the primary challenges for social transition are at school and at extended family gatherings. One key indicator of readiness for a social transition is the child's sense that the relief from being true to herself will outweigh any harassment she may encounter. It is difficult to know in advance the amount of harassment your child may experience. Many parents expect harassment to increase when a child makes a social transition. In my experience, however, many kids who had been harassed earlier for being gender nonconforming were treated better once they became confident about making a social transition. An increasingly androgynous presentation (masculine attire and manner) by the teen prior to the transition will give you some ability to anticipate the likely level of harassment and plan accordingly.

**Making the social transition**

The following steps have helped my clients accomplish the social transition more smoothly:

- Your teen will begin by informing close friends that she is a boy. She will gradually dress in a more androgynous manner if she has not already done so. She will find that friends who have already shown themselves to be accepting of gays, lesbians, and gender nonconforming people are likely to be most supportive. If your teen has previously come out as lesbian, she will already know which of her peers are open-minded regarding these matters. (As mentioned in Chapter 4, some transgender people go through a phase of identifying as gay or lesbian.)

- Next, you and your teen will meet with school administrators (or perhaps first with a sympathetic teacher or guidance counselor) to request the transition. If there is a GSA (Gay

Straight Alliance) or similar LGBT support organization at your child's school, the group's advisor is a good person to contact first. You and your child will explain that she is transsexual. You may have to explain to administrators what that means. You will request that she be viewed as male at school and addressed by her chosen male name and male pronouns.

• You will request that the school take whatever steps it deems necessary to assure more open-mindedness about gender diversity (such as presentations for students and/or faculty by a diversity advocacy group) and to guarantee, to the greatest extent possible, that you child is safe at school and will be treated with respect. If your school administration's response is unsatisfactory, a good resource to call on is Trans Youth Family Allies (*www.imatyfa.org*). Any LGBT youth organizations in your region, such as the wonderful True Colors, in Connecticut (*www.ourtruecolors.org*), can provide valuable assistance. It is the school administration's responsibility to assure that teachers and students will be educated about gender diversity, that teachers will honor the student's gender identity and that harassment will not be tolerated.

• The school will need to decide on a bathroom for the teen to use (usually a single bathroom such as in the nurse's office) and make provisions for changing and showering for gym class or sports.

• Generally, word of mouth along with your teen's answers to friendly questions about her male presentation will suffice to orient the rest of the student body to the new gender.

While this process has worked repeatedly for the teens who have been my clients, it is important to discuss with your teen what approach would make her most comfortable. You should discuss with the school administration (with sympathetic staff included in the discussion), what steps they believe will achieve the smoothest transition. Then get ready to take it in stride when your daughter's friends call, asking for her by her male name, or teachers tell you what a pleasure it is to have *him* in their class.

You may discover that school personnel have many of the same fears and concerns you and other parents have experienced (see Chapter 6). Be patient and persistent in encouraging them to address these fears and concerns. Ask them to keep in mind that your child's welfare depends on her ability to make the social transition. If you encounter extreme hostility at any point in this process, you and your child may also decide that alternate schooling is the best and safest choice. It will not be best for your daughter to abandon her need to be her authentic male self if that path becomes more difficult. If that should happen, just pull back, reassess your options, and find another way to move forward.

## Informing family and friends

Telling the extended family and friends of the family is a stressful experience for most parents of transgender teens. Fear of rejection and criticism, or fear of causing unmanageable distress for older family members is common. Many families keep this matter secret until a family or social gathering is coming. My recommendation to teens is that they defer to their parents, whenever possible, on notifying the relatives and adult family friends. My recommendation to parents is that they begin early on disclosing to close family and friends that their daughter is questioning her gender identity. This lays the groundwork for a later disclosure of the new male identity. As with your teen's disclosures, you will get the best responses from those who have already indicated in some way that they are open minded about LGBT people. Start with them first.

When it comes time for your child's social transition, it is important that you be in charge of how this information is shared with the extended family. In my experience, families have accomplished this by direct phone calls to each individual if the network is not that large, or by a letter or email if calling everyone is unmanageable. I do not recommend taking the short cut of asking one person to tell another, unless the intermediary knows your child well and is well-versed in information about transsexuals.

By the time you are ready to send this letter, you will have gained some comfort and consistency in using your child's male name and using male pronouns. This will be reflected in the way you write your letter. Notice that I use male pronouns in the following suggestions for the letter to extended family and friends. I will continue to use male pronouns, and also refer to your teen as your son, for the remainder of this chapter. Hopefully you will find this helpful, rather than confusing, as you continue to ponder what it means for your child to be transgender.

Your may want to include some or all of the following points in your letter:

- Tell family and friends that you would like them to receive some important news about your teen with an open mind. Let them know as simply and clearly as you can that you have learned something new about your child's identity. Share the new name and ask that they be respectful and make every effort to use this name and male pronouns when they speak to or about your child.

- Explain that while your child's new gender was difficult for you to accept at first, you now know that this transition is best for your teen and will lead to the happiest outcome for him and for the family. You may add that this is something he has struggled with for a long time in silence. You are proud of his courage and glad he is finally able to be true to himself.

- Stress that he is the same person he was when they knew him as a girl, with all of the same positive attributes you all value and love. (Don't hesitate to mention what those wonderful characteristics are!)

- Let them know that you welcome any questions they have about this change and that you look forward to telling them more about this if they would like to know more. You can also recommend this book to them so they can become more familiar with what it means to be transgender.

Be sure to review the letter with your teen before you send it out so he is comfortable with what you have written. Your teen may want to send a separate letter, or include a personal message in yours.

Here, as an example, is the letter sent by Cassie's parents. (See Cassie's story in Chapter 5):

Dear Friends and Family,

We have some news to share with you. There's been a big change in our family! Over the past year our easygoing Cassie had suddenly turned angry and uncooperative. We couldn't understand why until she told us that she really feels she is a boy and not a girl. It turns out she has been feeling out of place as a girl for a long time. This idea that Cassie is really a boy was hard for us to accept, and I imagine it will be hard for you, too.

Perhaps you have heard or read news stories about kids who are transgender, who make a transition at school from girl to boy or vice versa. We have been learning all about it since Cassie told us about herself. Since Cassie has accepted herself as transgender, she is back to being the same easygoing kid she always was – except now she is a smart, easygoing, athletic *boy*. His new name is Marcus. I hope you'll make the change to calling him Marcus and thinking of him as a boy, as we have. It definitely takes some practice! In fact, we're amazed that his friends and teachers are getting used to it, too.

We've met other transgender kids and their parents. It's been a big help to feel we're not alone with this. And now we want to invite you to be part of this big change in our lives. Please feel free to call or visit, to ask Marcus and us any questions you have. We're counting on your support!

Fondly,

For another example, see Chapter 8 for the letter sent by Sam's parents. (Sam's story is in Chapter 4.)

**Other steps in the social transition**

Along with changing name, pronouns, clothes and grooming, transboys will most likely want to purchase a chest binder, which is a garment, available online, that safely and comfortably flattens the breasts so he can more easily pass as a boy. A transsexual youth may request a legal name change when he feels certain of his intent to make a full and permanent transition. This can generally be accomplished through your local probate court. If your child has made a social transition and legal name change, your gender identity therapist can help provide documentation, per your state's regulations, to have the gender marker on his driver's license changed to male. Having identification that is consistent with his gender presentation helps protect your teenager from harassment and keeps his transgender status private.

# Hormones

There are two types of hormonal intervention that can be offered to teenagers: puberty-blocking hormones and cross-gender hormones.

**Puberty-blocking hormones**

Puberty-blocking hormones are given to teens in the early stages of puberty who have met the following criteria:

- They have been gender nonconforming since childhood,
- They have completed 6 months of psychotherapy, and
- They have already made a social transition or feel that they are likely to want to do so.

These hormones suspend the bodily changes of puberty, giving the teen more time to decide on a future course. If by age 16 or 17 your biologically female teen who has been taking puberty-blocking hormones determines that his gender is male, then he can initiate cross-gender hormones with a better physical (male) outcome than if he had gone through female puberty before transitioning. Since he will be able to avoid breast development through the use of puberty-blocking hormones, he will not need to wear a binder or have breast removal surgery should he continue on the path toward male adulthood. If, however, your teen concludes that she is *not* transsexual, the puberty-blocking hormones are discontinued and she will experience a delayed but otherwise normal female puberty.

**Cross-gender hormones**

Cross-gender hormones are the second category of hormones. These can be given to teens as young as 16 years old, according to the Standards of Care.[4] These hormones (primarily testosterone for female-to-male) allow the body to conform more closely to the individual's gender identity. Many transsexual teens feel some emotional relief immediately upon starting to take hormones, although the desired physical changes (facial hair, lower voice and increased upper body strength for FTM) will take some months to begin and a number of years to reach completion. Taking cross-gender hormones creates certain medical risks and may lead to infertility. These are matters which the teen and his parents

---

[4] If your child is not old enough or in some other way is not ready for cross-gender hormones, you can speak to the pediatrician about medication to stop menstruation. This intervention may be appropriate for the female to male child who is highly distressed by menstrual periods because of gender identity.

must discuss with the gender identity therapist before a referral is made to an endocrinologist knowledgeable about cross-gender hormones. These concerns will be discussed further with the endocrinologist and relevant lab tests will be done before your teen can start taking hormones.

Your son will have to take cross-gender hormones throughout his life if he wants all of the changes caused by the hormones to persist. The medical risks will also persist as long as he is taking hormones. Therefore it is essential that your son maintains regular visits with the endocrinologist and completes all lab tests as requested to maintain the highest level of medical safety. It is important to take the prescribed dose exactly as directed by the doctor. It is not safe to seek hormones without a doctor's prescription. Your child's gender identity therapist will help you and your teen think through the hormone options, clarify when hormone treatment may be indicated, and make a referral to an appropriate physician at your request.

**Impatient teens**

Many transgender teens are exceedingly anxious to begin taking hormones, long before their parents have enough information to consider such a request, or the confidence that such intervention is right for their child. You will have to ask your teen to be patient as you take the time you need to understand his identity, his needs, and the realities of hormonal intervention. In most cases, a 3 or 6 month delay in starting hormones will not make an appreciable difference in long term outcome. (Exceptions to this would be a child experiencing rapid onset of puberty, or a teen who wants to start hormones during his senior year of high school to be able to pass better as male when he starts college.) I often point out to impatient teens that they are well ahead of the pack in that they have reached a clear understanding of their gender discordance and have parents who are engaged in this process with them. Most transsexuals have had to wait well into adulthood to have the understanding and resources to transition, and many have done so without any support or acceptance from their families.

# Surgery

Surgery for the purpose of having one's body conform to one's gender identity is not done prior to the age of 18. If your teen is requesting surgery, he will generally need your agreement and support (financial and otherwise) if he is to have surgery done in young adulthood. The most common surgery sought by young adults is "top surgery" (double mastectomy) for FTM. This surgery relieves the transboy who has made a social transition from having to continue to use a binder and keep his chest covered all summer. He no longer has to walk stooped over or wear loose, layered clothes to hide his breasts. For parents, the idea of this surgery can be quite disturbing, even if it is something your child deeply desires. It is important to take the time you need to understand that your son is extremely uncomfortable about having female breasts. It may help if you imagine how a conventionally male child would feel if he developed breasts in puberty. While your teen may be happy about the prospect of surgery, you may need time to grieve the loss of a cherished daughter. Keep in mind that for a long time he has not felt that he is a daughter. When you are ready, he needs to be cherished as your son. Most of the things you value and admire about him will be unchanged. He is likely after surgery to be happier and more at ease, more comfortable in his body.

Additional surgeries that are generally delayed at least until your teen is well into his 20s will not be discussed in any detail here. These include genital surgery and hysterectomy. Genital surgery is sought less often by FTMs because the results are not yet as satisfactory as they are for MTFs. The decision regarding hysterectomy for gender transition (discomfort with having female organs) is a complex matter. Both of these surgeries are steps which your young person is likely to take only after he is well into young adulthood, so your role as a parent in the process may be quite different at that point.

# CHAPTER TEN

# CONCLUSION

*The key thing that we need to remember is that our son will be fine – healthy,*
*secure, happy and successful. I worry about a lot of things, but not about*
*that. He has a great life in front of him, full of friends and accomplishments.*
*And behind him, he has a loving family. That's a pretty solid foundation,*
*no matter what hardships he might face, or what victories he might celebrate.*
– Parent of a transboy in a letter to friends and family.

Now it's time to take a deep breath and reflect on all you have
read here. It will also be helpful to talk things over with your spouse
or partner, close friends or family, and your child. You may want to
confer with a mental health professional or clergy. Thinking about
surgery can be especially upsetting, so let go of that for now.

**Keep an open mind**

Focus on what's most important at this time:

- Keep an open mind about the validity and meaning of your
  child's inner experience.  Remember that keeping an open

mind about what your child is telling you keeps the lines of communication open.

- Examine your fears and concerns. It is natural for parents, because of their fears and concerns, to have a bias against believing that a child may be transsexual. But if your first response is to strongly oppose what your teen is saying about gender identity, he or she is more likely to adopt a stubborn, oppositional point of view in future discussions.

- Listen, ask questions, be flexible, be patient.

## Wrapping up

It is wonderful for your child that you are willing to face this difficult situation head on. I know you want to be the best support you can be for your teen. You also want to keep your child safe. At times your child may be impatient and angry with you for having doubts or taking too much time. At those times, be sure to appreciate your own efforts, and your willingness to proceed on this challenging path. With an open mind, compassion and perseverance you and your teen will find your way to a positive outcome.

The final chapter of this book is a list of resources to help you gain a greater understanding of your teen. I have also listed organizations you can turn to for support for yourself and for your child as you begin to take steps. Remember to take your time and to take advantage of all of the resources available. Remember, also, that many other families have faced these challenges with remarkably good outcomes.

In my work, I am inspired every day by my transgender clients. They are willing to overcome tremendous obstacles in order to be completely true to themselves. I hope this book will help you appreciate and support your transgender teen in his or her struggle to achieve full authenticity.

# CHAPTER ELEVEN

# RESOURCES FOR PARENTS OF TRANSGENDER TEENS

## Advocacy, Research and Support Organizations in the U.S.

**Family Acceptance Project** (*http://familyproject.sfsu.edu*) is a community research, intervention and education initiative to study the impact of family acceptance and rejection on the health, mental health and well-being of LGBT youth.

**The Gay, Lesbian and Straight Education Network** (GLSEN) (*www.glsen.org*) is the largest national education organization working to ensure safe schools for all students.

**Parents and Friends of Lesbians and Gays** (PFLAG) (*www.pflag.org*). In 2002, the PFLAG Transgender Network (TNET) became PFLAG's first "Special Affiliate." TNET is focused specifically on promoting the health and well-being of transgender persons, their families and friends.

**Trans Youth Family Allies** (TYFA) (*www.imatyfa.org*) empowers children and families by partnering with educators, service providers and communities, to develop supportive environments in which gender may be expressed and respected. The website has good information about advocating for your child.

**Transgender Law and Policy Institute** (*www.transgenderlaw.org*) and the **Transgender Law Center** (*www.transgenderlawcenter.org*) provide legal advocacy for transgender people. They are located in New York and California, respectively.

**The Trevor Project** (*www.thetrevorproject.org*): 888-4-U-TREVOR is a free and confidential 24/7 crisis and suicide prevention helpline for LGBT youth.

**Trevor Space** (*www.trevorspace.org*) is a free, monitored social and peer networking site for LGBT youth ages 13-24.

# Organizations Providing Youth Conferences, Advocacy, Training and Education in the U.S.

**Gender Spectrum** (*www.genderspectrum.org*) provides education, training and support to help create a gender sensitive and inclusive environment for all children and teens. Gender Spectrum is located in California.

**True Colors** (*www.ourtruecolors.org*) works with other social service agencies, schools, organizations, and within communities to meet the needs of sexual and gender minority youth. The organization trains more than 2400 people annually, organizes the largest LGBT youth conference in the country and manages the state's only LGBT mentoring program. True Colors is located in Connecticut.

# Listservs (email-based groups for sharing support and information)

**TransFamily** (*www.transfamily.org/emailist.htm*) hosts listservs and also provides information and support.

**Washington DC Children's National Medical Center** (*www.child-rensnational.org/gendervariance*). Contact *pgroup@cnmc.org* to join the email list for parents of gender nonconforming children and teens.

# Counseling

These web sites may help you find a therapist in your area who is experienced in the treatment of transgender persons:

- Dr. Becky Allison: *www.drbecky.com/therapists.html.*

- Laura's Playground: *www.laurasplayground.com/gender_therapists.htm*

- The World Professional Association for Transgender Health *www.wpath.org.* From the home page click on "find a provider" then just enter your State (if you are in the U.S.) and click on "submit."

If possible, it is best to verify independently that the therapist you find is fully credentialed and licensed. You can do this by speaking with a local health care provider.

# Organizations Outside the U.S.

Canada: **Vancouver Coastal Health** (*http://transhealth.vch.ca*). This website provides extensive information about transgender health.

Australia: **True Colours** (*www.truecolours.org.au*). This organization represents young transsexuals and their parents, families and supporters.

United Kingdom: **Mermaids** (*www.mermaidsuk.org.uk*) is a support group originally formed in 1995 by a group of parents who were brought together as a result of their children's longstanding gender identity issues.

# Books and Other Written Materials

*The Transgender Child* by Stephanie Brill and Rachel Pepper, Cleis Press, 2008.

*True Selves: Understanding Transsexualism* by Mildred L. Brown and Chloe Ann Rounsley, Jossey-Bass, 1996.

*The Sexual Spectrum: Why We're All Different* by Olive Skene Johnson, Raincoast Books, 2004.

Novels:
    *Luna* by Julie Anne Peters, Little, Brown and Company, 2004
    *Parrotfish* by Ellen Wittlinger, Simon and Schuster, 2007.

*Bending the Mold: an action kit for transgender students,* available from *www.lambdalegal.org.*

*Beyond the Binary: a toolkit for gender identity activism in schools,* available from *www.gsanetwork.org.*

# Additional References Used for this Book

"Eligibility and Readiness Criteria for Sex Reassignment Surgery: Recommendations for Revision of the WPATH *Standards of Care,*" Griet de Cuypere and Herman Vercruysse, Jr., *International Journal of Transgenderism,* 11:3, July-September 2009, pp. 194- 205.

"Medical Care for Gender Variant Young People: Dealing with the Practical Problems," B.W.D. Reed, P.T. Cohen-Kettinis, T. Reed, and N. Spack, *Sexologies,* 17:4, October – December 2008, pp. 258-264.

"Review of World Professional Association for Transgender Health's Standards of Care for Children and Adolescents with Gender Identity Disorder: A Need for Change?" Annelou L.C. DeVries and Peggy T. Cohen-Kettinis, *International Journal of Transgenderism,* 11:2, April – June 2009, pp. 100-109.

"Serving LGBT Youth in Out-of-Home Care," Child Welfare League of America Best Practices Guidelines, 2006.

"Supportive Families, Healthy Children: Helping Families with Lesbian, Gay, Bisexual and Transgender Children," Caitlin Ryan, PhD, Family Acceptance Project, 2009.

*Transgenderism and Intersexuality in Childhood and Adolescence; Making Choices* by Peggy T. Cohen-Kettenis and Friedmann Pfafflin, Sage Publications, 2003.

# GLOSSARY

*Affirmed female* is a person with a male body who considers herself female.

*Affirmed gender identity* is the gender identity that a person has declared to others.

*Affirmed male* is a person with a female body who considers himself male.

*Androgynous* presentation includes both masculine and feminine elements.

*Authenticity*, in this book, is the quality of being true to oneself and presenting one's true self to others.

*Biological sex*, male or female, is assigned at birth based on the appearance of the baby's genitals.

*Bisexual* individuals feel love and sexual attraction toward males and females.

*Clinical social worker* is a psychotherapist with an advanced degree in Social Work.

*Coming out* is the process of telling others that one is gay, lesbian, bisexual or transgender.

*Conventionally gendered* individuals' biological sex, gender identity and gender expression are either all male or all female.

*Cross-gender hormones* cause a male body to become more female or a female body to become more male.

*Crossdressers* wish to adopt the clothing and styles of grooming typical, in their culture, of the other sex.

*Effeminate* boys are those whose manner and behavior are highly feminine.

*Electrolysis* is a treatment to remove unwanted facial or body hair.

*Endocrinologist* is a physician specializing in the body's production of hormones, including those that make a person more masculine or feminine.

*Facial feminization* is surgery to make a masculine face appear feminine.

*Female-to-Male* (FTM) transsexual has a female body, is considered by others to be female, but feels male. He wants to have a male body and to be viewed by others as male.

*Gay* is a common term for homosexual.

*Gay male* refers to men who love and are sexually attracted to men.

*Gender discordance* is the experience of having a gender identity that differs from one's biological sex.

*Gender dysphoria* is a clinical term used to describe the unhappiness caused by the conflict between gender identity and biological sex or societal expectations for that sex.

*Gender expression or Gender presentation* is a person's presentation of self to others as masculine, feminine, neither or both.

*Gender identity* is a person's inner sense of being female, male, neither or both.

*Gender identity therapist* is a mental health professional with expertise about gender identity and expression.

*Gender nonconforming* kids are those whose desires, behaviors and manner do not conform to what society expects from children of their biological sex.

*Genderfluid* or *Genderqueer* people are those with a gender identity that is neither male nor female, or is a blend of male and female.

*Heterosexual* individuals feel love and sexual attraction toward members of the opposite sex.

*Homosexual* individuals feel love and sexual attraction toward members of the same sex.

*Intersex* people have genitals that are not exclusively male or female.

*LGBT* is an abbreviation for lesbian, gay, bisexual and transgender.

*Lesbian* refers to women who love and are sexually attracted to women.

*Male-to-Female* (MTF) transsexual has a male body, is considered by others to be male, but feels female. She wants to have a female body and to be viewed by others as female.

*Pansexual* individuals feel love and sexual attraction toward others without placing importance on the partner's sex or gender.

*Psychotherapy* is counseling to address mental health or substance abuse problems.

*Puberty* is the stage of physical development when an individual's body undergoes sexual maturation.

*Puberty-blocking hormones* postpone the onset of puberty.

*Sex*, female or male, is assigned at birth based on the appearance of the baby's genitals.

*Sexual orientation* refers to the type of sexual attractions a person feels. Gay, lesbian, straight and bisexual are examples of sexual orientations.

*Sexuality* refers to sexual feelings and behaviors.

*Social transition* is the time when a transsexual person begins presenting in public according to his or her gender identity rather than according to his or her biological sex.

*Straight* is a common term for heterosexual.

*Transboy* is a child or adolescent female-to male transsexual.

*Transgender* people have a gender identity and/or gender expression that does not conform to the sex of their body.

*Transgenderism* is the body of knowledge on the subject of being transgender.

*Transgirl* is a child or adolescent male-to-female transsexual.

*Transition*, in this book, refers to the process of changing from male to female or female to male.

*Transsexuals* are people whose gender identity is in sharp contrast to their biological sex.

CPSIA information can be obtained at www.ICGtesting.com
Printed in the USA
BVOW08s1921131113

336240BV00005B/303/P